Holes

L-I-T *Guide*
Literature In Teaching

By Louis Sachar

A Study Guide for Grades 4 to 8
Prepared by Barbara T. Doherty and Charlotte S. Jaffe
Illustrated by Karen Sigler

ISBN 1-56644-063-7

EDUCATIONAL IMPRESSIONS, INC.
Hawthorne, NJ 07507

Printed in the United States of America.

This study guide is based on the book *Holes*
Copyright © 1998 by Louis Sachar
Published by Farrar, Straus and Giroux, New York

Holes
Written by Louis Sachar

STORY SUMMARY

Stanley and his family have been cursed with "bad luck" for several generations. It started with Stanley's great-great-grandfather in Europe. Accusing him of stealing a pig from her, a gypsy woman put a curse on Stanley's great-great-grandfather and his descendants. Bad luck is one thing, but being sent to prison camp because a pair of old sneakers falls out of the sky onto you is quite something else! But this is exactly what happened to Stanley Yelnats IV.

Camp Green Lake was in the middle of an empty desert. There had once been a town of Green Lake and, of course, the lake itself. But these had disappeared a long time ago. It was a perfect place for a detention camp. There was no sign of civilization nearby. Fences were not needed, as escape would be foolish. The only water supply was at the camp. The desert was home to rattlesnakes, scorpions, and deadly, poisonous lizards. As punishment, the Warden insisted that each boy dig a hole each day. The hole had to be 5-feet deep and five-feet in any direction. Although she said that it was to build character, she had ulterior motives. The Warden was a vicious woman. She ruled with an iron fist and expected immediate obedience.

The boys all had prison names. Stanley was given the name of Caveman within a few days. Caveman tried to adapt to the heat, the poor food, the loss of family, the physical demands of digging, and the fear. He found his first real friend in Zero, a fellow "camper." When Zero ran away, Caveman knew that Zero would not be able to survive alone. Caveman ran away to help his friend.

A series of flashbacks ties the present to the past. Finally, the mystery is solved and the Yelnats' luck seems to change for the better.

Meet the Author
Louis Sachar

Born in East Meadow, New York, on March 20, 1954, Louis Sachar moved with his family to Tustin, California, when he was nine. As a child, Louis enjoyed reading and playing Little League baseball. E. B. White was his favorite author.

Louis briefly attended Antioch College in Ohio but returned to California at the time of his father's death. After a short career as a Fuller Brush salesman, he resumed his college education at the University of California, Berkeley. By chance, he learned of a part-time job as a teacher's aid in a nearby elementary school. For his efforts there, he received college credits. "With much reluctance, I ended up doing the job. Now I've become a children's book writer because of that experience," Sachar later recalled. In 1976, the author earned a BA degree from the university.

Sachar decided to continue his education by becoming a lawyer. He attended Hastings College of Law in San Francisco. While attending law school, he began writing *Sideways Stories from the Wayside School.* These stories were based on his experiences as a teacher's aid. Sachar received his Doctors of Laws degree in 1980 but continued to write children's books in his spare time. In 1989, he decided to give up the practice of law to devote all his time to writing. He married in 1985.

In addition to using his childhood experiences in his stories, the author also uses his daughter as his inspiration. In the *Marvin Redpost* series, Marvin's four-year-old sister is modeled after Sachar's daughter. When Sachar does his writing, he prefers to be alone. "It took me a year to write *There's a Boy in the Girls' Bathroom.* I wrote it alone in my room, keeping it all to myself, not letting anyone know about it. I always hoped kids would like it."

Sachar has received recognition for many of his popular children's books. His *Sideways Stories from the Wayside School* was named a Children's Choice book in 1979. *There's a Boy in the Girls' Bathroom* was given the Mark Twain and Milner Awards, among others. *Holes* was the recipient of the prestigious Newbery Medal and the National Book Award. Sachar enjoys writing for children. "I want kids to think that reading can be just as much fun and more so than TV or video games or whatever else they do." The author now resides in Austin, Texas, where he enjoys softball, chess, and rugby.

Pre-Reading Information
Onions

Red, yellow, white, or green onions are grown and enjoyed all over the world. There are over five hundred different varieties! It is truly one of the world's most popular vegetables. Onions belong to the genus *Allium*. Other members are leeks, chives, garlic, and scallions.

It is believed that onions were first used as a food in central Asia. By way of the ancient trade routes, the onion spread throughout the Roman Empire. The Romans named this flavorful bulb *unio*. Later, the word became *oinyon* in England in the Middle Ages.

Low in sodium, onions contain potassium, several B vitamins, and vitamin C. The health properties of onions have been known for a long time. Onion juice was rubbed on the muscles of athletes in ancient Greece. These same athletes were encouraged to eat onions to improve their blood. During the Middle Ages, Europeans relied on onions to cure many ailments, including headaches, snakebites, and even balding.

Onions are easy to grow and cheap to buy. They store well and are available year round. "Know your onions" is an old expression meaning to be aware of how life works and how to get the most out of it.

Vocabulary

Chapters 1, 2, 3, 4, & 5

Use the words in the box to complete the following sentences. You may need to use your dictionary.

alert	**canteen**	**convicted**	**counselor**	**dazed**
embarrassment	**facilities**	**forbidden**	**gruff**	**hammock**
obstacle	**perseverance**	**premises**	**vast**	

1. The children are ________________ to play in the street.
2. Maria found it difficult to stay ________________ when driving late at night.
3. The ________________ criminal was sentenced to a long jail term.
4. Several new ________________ will be added to the campground next year.
5. The school ________________ helped the students select courses of study.
6. My ________________ needed to be refilled with fresh water.
7. Samantha seemed a bit ________________ by the bright sunlight.
8. The bad-tempered man spoke in a ________________ voice.
9. A(n) ________________ mountain range loomed before us.
10. Because of a(n) ________________ on the roadway, the traffic became clogged.
11. Ben relaxed on the ________________ as it swayed between two trees.
12. Stanley suffered from ________________ when his teacher used him as an example.
13. At Camp Green Lake, no alcohol was allowed on the ________________.
14. Through ________________, Peter finally learned to swim.

If only, if only…

The Yelnats family endures bad luck. Tell about a time when you weren't so lucky. Use some vocabulary words from the first part of this activity.

Comprehension and Discussion Questions

Chapters 1, 2, 3, 4, & 5

Answer the following questions in complete sentence form. Give examples from the story to support your response.

1. Why was Camp Green Lake an unlikely name for the place where Stanley was sent? What name would you have given it instead? Judge Stanley's decision to go to Camp Green Lake. If you were Stanley, what choice would you have made? Explain.

2. Why did some campers welcome a scorpion or rattlesnake bite?

3. A gypsy woman had put a curse on Elya Yelnats and his descendants. Although they did not believe in curses, Stanley and his father—like their descendants—were plagued by bad luck. Do you agree with Stanley's mother that Stanley's great-grandfather, the first Stanley Yelnats, was lucky? Explain.

4. Why wasn't it necessary to have fences at Camp Green Lake?

5. Explain Mr. Pendanski's reason for refusing to call the boys by their nicknames. In your opinion, how did the boys get their nicknames?

Vocabulary

Chapters 6 & 7

Match the vocabulary words on the left to the definitions on the right. Place the correct letter on each line.

____ 1. aimlessly	A. shortage
____ 2. assure	B. having a flaw
____ 3. automatically	C. facial expression
____ 4. coincidence	D. to lower someone's pride
____ 5. defective	E. distance around an area
____ 6. desperate	F. a sequence of accidental events that seem planned
____ 7. envious	G. having lost all hope; despairing
____ 8. eternity	H. done without purpose
____ 9. expelled	I. jealous
____ 10. grimace	J. to get back; to regain
____ 11. humiliate	K. done in a manner free from external control
____ 12. mutter	L. an unoccupied position or place of accommodation
____ 13. perimeter	M. forced out
____ 14. reluctant	N. to inform confidently
____ 15. retrieve	O. to speak indistinctly in low tones
____ 16. scarcity	P. unwilling
____ 17. vacancy	Q. a seemingly endless time

Lullaby

Write a second verse to the pig lullaby that Sarah sang. Use some of the vocabulary words from the first part of the activity in your song.

____

____

____

____

Comprehension and Discussion Questions

Chapters 6 & 7

Answer the following questions in complete sentence form. Give examples from the story to support your response.

1. Why did the boys doubt Stanley's reason for being sent to Camp Green Lake? What was ironic about the situation?

2. Describe Stanley's mixed feelings about meeting Clyde Livingston. How would you have felt if you were Stanley?

3. Explain the reason that Stanley's crime was labeled despicable by the judge. If you were the judge, what verdict would you have reached in Stanley's case?

4. Elya had refused to pick a number and he had stated, "Marry Igor, you can keep my pig as a wedding present." If you were Elya, what choice would you have made? What does this story have to do with the main story about Stanley?

5. Why did Sarah and Elya Yelnats name their child Stanley?

Vocabulary

Chapters 8, 9, 10, 11, & 12

Define the following words according to their use in the story.

1. **appropriate** ______________________
2. **arced** ______________________
3. **commercial** ______________________
4. **fossilized** ______________________
5. **glared** ______________________
6. **obviously** ______________________
7. **predatory** ______________________
8. **radiated** ______________________
9. **referred** ______________________
10. **scowl** ______________________
11. **smug** ______________________
12. **veterinarian** ______________________

Alliteration Creations

Alliteration is the literary device that is used by authors for a special effect. It is the repetition of the initial or beginning sound in two or more words in a sentence.

Example: Stanley was surprised to see such a stark setting.

Use the words from the first part of the activity to create your own alliteration sentences that relate to a story character or event.

Comprehension and Discussion Questions

Chapters 8, 9, 10, 11, & 12

Answer the following questions in complete sentence form. Give examples from the story to support your response.

1. Explain the pun used in naming the boys' recreation area.

2. Examine Stanley's incomplete letter to his mother. It was written in a positive tone. Which items in it were actually true? Which were not?

3. In what way did Stanley's interesting discovery turn out to be a disappointment? Were you surprised at Mr. Pendanski's reaction?

4. Judge Mr. Pendanski's statement to Stanley: "You're responsible for yourself. You messed up your life, and it's up to you to fix it. No one else is going to do it for you." Explain your reasons for agreeing or disagreeing with the statement.

5. Why was it surprising that X-Ray was the leader?

Vocabulary

Chapters 13, 14, & 15

For each sentence below, circle the most appropriate definition for the word in bold as it is used in the sentence. Use your dictionary to help you.

1. Mr. Andrews is an **authority** on rare coins.

   collector expert writer

2. Pandora's **curiosity** got the best of her, so she opened her box.

   anger inquisitiveness jealousy

3. The workers **excavated** the remains of the ancient city.

   sighted buried dug

4. The stars **glistened** in the clear night sky.

   appeared dimmed sparkled

5. Because of the **haze**, we could not see the distant mountain range.

   rain storm cloudiness

6. Mrs. Connor carefully dusted her **precious** antique vase.

   pretty popular valuable

7. The cook **sifted** the sugar on the top of the pastry.

   strained spread replaced

8. Stanley wondered if Zigzag was a bit **paranoid** when he said that the boys were being watched.

   silly distrustful careful

9. The jeweler **engraved** the girl's initials on her new bracelet.

   attached designed carved

10. Due to foggy conditions, the ocean was not **visible** in the morning.

    navigable seen rough

Comprehension and Discussion Questions

Chapters 13, 14, & 15

Answer the following questions in complete sentence form. Give examples from the story to support your response.

1. Judge whether Stanley made the correct decision when he surrendered his find to X-Ray. What did X-Ray do for Stanley in return? Explain what you might have done in Stanley's place.

____

____

____

____

2. Characterize the Warden. Guess why she wanted the canteens refilled.

____

____

____

____

3. What caused Stanley to realize that they weren't just digging to build character—that they were definitely looking for something?

____

____

____

____

4. Why didn't X-Ray want to talk to Stanley about the gold tube at breakfast?

____

____

____

____

5. Do you have any idea what the KB might stand for?

____

____

____

____

Vocabulary

Chapters 16, 17, 18, & 19

Use your dictionary to define the following words as they are used in the chapters.

1. **allergies** ____________________
2. **blankly** ____________________
3. **burlap** ____________________
4. **callused** ____________________
5. **exhaust** ____________________
6. **gash** ____________________
7. **Hispanic** ____________________
8. **intently** ____________________
9. **obstacle** ____________________
10. **penetrating** ____________________
11. **presumably** ____________________
12. **sprawled** ____________________

Dear Diary

Pretend that Stanley is keeping a diary of his experiences at Camp Green Lake. Choose an episode from Chapter 16, 17, 18, or 19 that would make a good diary entry. Tell about it using four or more vocabulary words from the first part of this activity.

Dear Diary,

Comprehension and Discussion Questions

Chapters 16, 17, 18, & 19

Answer the following questions in complete sentence form. Give examples from the story to support your response.

1. What was ironic about the Warden's statement: "Glad you're here X-Ray. We need your sharp eyes"?

2. In general, Stanley's experience at Camp Green Lake was a difficult one. How was it beneficial to him?

3. Describe the change in the Warden's personality. Explain the reason for the change.

4. Judge Stanley's refusal to help Zero learn to read and write.

5. What event caused Stanley to realize that he was again in the wrong place at the wrong time? How did Stanley deal with the problem? How would you have dealt with the same situation?

Vocabulary

Chapters 20, 21, 22, 23, & 24

Choose the word in each set that is **most like** the first word in meaning.

1. **agony**	pleasure	sensitivity	pain
2. **condemn**	shorten	join	blame
3. **defiance**	cooperation	consent	insolence
4. **desolate**	forlorn	envious	hopeful
5. **disrespectful**	controlling	rude	friendly
6. **dread**	optimism	satisfaction	fear
7. **fabulous**	extraordinary	radical	pleasant
8. **grotesque**	balanced	distorted	fancy
9. **jolt**	shock	prank	taunt
10. **recede**	advance	withdraw	promote
11. **remote**	nearby	midway	distant
12. **shrill**	soft	piercing	wavering
13. **toxic**	poisonous	mild	clear
14. **violent**	fierce	gentle	careless

Use three words from this activity in sentences that describe characters or events in the story.

Comprehension and Discussion Questions

Chapters 20, 21, 22, 23, & 24

Answer the following questions in complete sentence form. Give examples from the story to support your response.

1. Explain the meaning of the Warden's statement: "He's not going to die. Unfortunately for you."

2. In your opinion, why did Stanley change his mind and decide to teach Zero to read and write after all?

3. What surprising fact did Stanley learn about Zero's abilities?

4. Judge Katherine Barlow's refusal to go for a boat ride with Trout. Do you think she made the correct choice? Explain your reasoning.

5. How did Mr. Sir get even with Stanley for the Warden's behavior?

Vocabulary

Chapters 25, 26, 27, & 28

Read each clue and find the answers in the box. Then use the letters above the numbered spaces to decipher the secret message. Not all words are used.

arthritis	**asthma**	**blotchy**	**concocts**	**digestion**	**drawl**
motorized	**ointment**	**outlaw**	**quivering**	**remedy**	
semester	**sparingly**	**waded**	**wobble**		

1. chronic breathing disease ___ ___(1) ___(2) ___ ___ ___(3)
2. solution to a problem ___ ___ ___ ___(6) ___ ___(7)
3. marked with spots or discolorations ___ ___(5) ___ ___ ___ ___(12) ___
4. move unsteadily ___ ___(20) ___ ___ ___ ___(9)
5. prepares; makes up ___(11) ___ ___ ___ ___ ___ ___(8) ___
6. substance used in healing ___(18) ___ ___ ___ ___ ___(13) ___ ___
7. walked through water ___ ___(23) ___ ___ ___(24)
8. changing of food in the body ___ ___ ___ ___ ___(14) ___(19) ___ ___ ___
9. part of a school year ___ ___(22) ___ ___(16) ___ ___ ___ ___
10. frugally ___ ___ ___(10) ___(21) ___ ___(4) ___ ___ ___
11. equipped with a motor ___ ___ ___ ___ ___(17) ___ ___(15) ___ ___

❂ *Secret Message* ❂

___ ___ ___ ___ ___ ___ ___   ___ ___ ___ ___ ___ ___ ___
1 2 3 4 5 6 7   8 9 10 11 12 13 14

___ ___ ___ ___   ___ ___   ___ ___ ___ ___ .
15 16 17 18   19 20   21 22 23 24

Comprehension and Discussion Questions

Chapters 25, 26, 27, & 28

Answer the following questions in complete sentence form. Give examples from the story to support your response.

1. Why did the people of Green Lake go to both Sam and Dr. Hawthorn for medical treatment? Why didn't Dr. Hawthorn resent this?

2. Summarize the events that turned Kate Barlow into a feared outlaw.

3. How did Mr. Pendanski show his kindness to Stanley?

4. What was Zero's real name? Where have we read the name?

5. Kate said to Trout, "You, and your children, and their children can dig for the next hundred years and you'll never find it." Guess if her prediction will come true. Explain.

Vocabulary

Chapters 29 & 30

Use the vocabulary words in the box to complete the sentences below. You may need to use your dictionary. Not all the words are used.

astonishment **awkward** **barren** **bravo** **cluster** **delirious** **depriving**

harsh **horizon** **humid** **pry** **refuge** **stress** **unconscious**

1. My friend's embarrassing remark made me feel very ________________ in front of the others.

2. The weather was ________________; it would be more comfortable if it were drier.

3. We took ________________ from the rain in the library.

4. Because he was rendered ________________ by the blow, Pete didn't remember being hit by the ball.

5. Not all the parts of the desert are ________________.

6. The ________________ wind was unpleasant as it hit our faces.

7. The children waited in a ________________ at the school entrance.

8. Large trees were ________________ the flower beds of sunlight.

9. ________________ may be caused by an overly busy day.

10. Jerry became ________________ upon learning that he had won the lottery; he could not control his emotions.

11. Marla stared in ________________ at the magician's amazing tricks.

12. The ship seemed to disappear as we looked out at the ________________.

13. When the performance ended, the audience shouted, "________________!"

14. The woman had to ________________ open the locked box with a stick.

Writing Activity

As Stanley, write a short letter home. Use at least four vocabulary words from the box.

Comprehension and Discussion Questions

Chapters 29 & 30

Answer the following questions in complete sentence form. Give examples from the story to support your response.

1. Why did Stanley keep thinking about what his great-grandfather had said after Kate Barlow had robbed him, "I found refuge on God's thumb." What do you think his great-grandfather had meant?

____

____

____

____

2. What caused Zero to hit Mr. Pendanski with the shovel?

____

____

____

____

3. Why did the Warden tell the counselors not to shoot Zero?

____

____

____

____

4. What did the Warden mean by the following: "It's almost time for me to paint my nails again"?

____

____

____

____

5. Predict who will dig the seventh hole.

____

____

____

____

Vocabulary

Chapters 31, 32, 33, & 34

Match the vocabulary words on the left to the definitions on the right. Place the correct letter on each line.

____ 1. accelerated	A. haphazard; having no specific pattern
____ 2. compound	B. compassion; leniency
____ 3. eventually	C. a handle used to operate a mechanism
____ 4. lever	D. a contest in which winners are determined by chance
____ 5. lottery	E. increased the speed
____ 6. lurched	F. moved briskly; mixed
____ 7. mercy	G. to remain alive or in existence
____ 8. mirage	H. finally; at last
____ 9. random	I. person under care or protection of a guardian or the court
____ 10. stirred	J. a building or buildings set off and enclosed by a barrier
____ 11. survive	K. an illusion; especially of water in a desert
____ 12. ward	L. moved suddenly

An antonym is a word that has an opposite meaning to that of another word. Choose five vocabulary words from the above activity. Write an antonym for each.

____

____

____

____

____

Comprehension and Discussion Questions

Chapters 31, 32, 33, & 34

Answer the following questions in complete sentence form. Give examples from the story to support your response.

1. Why did Stanley feel guilty about Zero's predicament?

2. Why did the Warden think that no one would question Zero's disappearance?

3. Judge Stanley's decision to try to take the truck to find Zero.

4. Why did Stanley revise his plan to walk until he was too weak to go any further and then return to camp?

5. What is interesting about the boat's name, *Mary Lou?*

Vocabulary

Chapters 35, 36 & 37

Read each sentence. Then circle the most appropriate definition for the word in **bold** as it is used in that sentence.

1. Ken could not guess the **altitude** of the kite.

   age — height — price

2. The soap was advertised to have anti-**bacteria** ingredients.

   aging — wrinkling — germs

3. Because of her cold, Carrie's voice sounded **raspy**.

   rough — soft — different

4. The orange juice had a **tangy** taste.

   hot — cold — sharp

5. Without rain, the garden was quickly **parched**.

   dormant — destroyed — dry

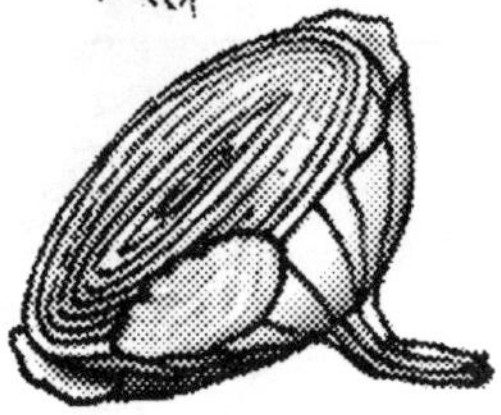

6. Butterflies are beautiful and **frail**.

   quiet — fragile — peaceful

7. We found the shovel **protruding** from the bushes.

   extending — separating — hiding

8. Mom **clutched** the baby as we rode down the bumpy path.

   fed — held — watched

9. Jim increased his savings in small **increments**.

   banks — cans — additions

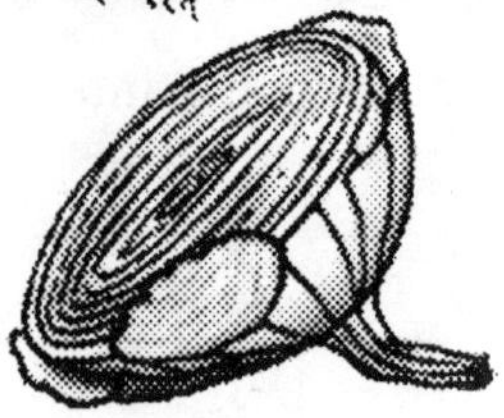

10. Ben **sheepishly** admitted his guilt in the prank.

    sorrowfully — proudly — timidly

Choose three vocabulary words from the above activity. Write an original sentence for each.

____

____

____

Comprehension and Discussion Questions

Chapters 35, 36 & 37

Answer the following questions in complete sentence form. Give examples from the story to support your response.

1. What do you think the "sploosh" really is? Why was it both a good and a bad discovery?

2. In what way did the spelling lessons help?

3. What bothered Stanley the most about the prospect of dying?

4. Stanley became more scared when he knew they would reach the mountain. Why? What caused him to feel somewhat relieved?

5. Find a simile in Chapter 35 that the author used to describe Zero's face. Find a metaphor in Chapter 36 that the author used to describe the sun.

Vocabulary

Chapters 38, 39, & 40

Use the vocabulary words in the box to create original sentences. When you have finished, rewrite the sentences, replacing each vocabulary word with a blank line. Only one vocabulary word should fit appropriately into each blank. You may use your dictionary. Exchange your missing-word sentences with a classmate to solve.

Example: It is important to include fruits and vegetables in your ____________.

Answer: diet

absorbed **contritely** **despair** **feebly** **foul** **gully** **leeches**

occasional **precipice** **snickers** **quack** **tonic**

Fill in the Blanks!

Sentences created by ______________________________

Sentences completed by ______________________________

1. ______________________________
2. ______________________________
3. ______________________________
4. ______________________________
5. ______________________________
6. ______________________________
7. ______________________________
8. ______________________________
9. ______________________________
10. ______________________________
11. ______________________________
12. ______________________________

Comprehension and Discussion Questions

Chapters 38, 39, & 40

Answer the following questions in complete sentence form. Give examples from the story to support your response.

1. To what did Stanley compare the first onion he found?

2. How did Zero and Stanley survive for the next few days?

3. What did Zero confess to Stanley? What hints did the author give us in past chapters that this might be the case?

4. In the flashback, what saved Rebecca Tennyson from dying? What did Mrs. Tennyson think caused the child's illness?

5. Why was Stanley surprised to find the shovel and the sack of jars so far down the mountain?

Vocabulary

Chapters 41, 42, & 43

Define the following vocabulary words. You may use your dictionary to help you.

1. **abruptly** ______
2. **adjacent** ______
3. **civilization** ______
4. **contaminate** ______
5. **crammed** ______
6. **declared** ______
7. **despite** ______
8. **destiny** ______
9. **diagram** ______
10. **evicted** ______
11. **fluttering** ______
12. **fugitive** ______
13. **identity** ______
14. **indistinct** ______
15. **inexplicable** ______
16. **murky** ______
17. **summoned** ______

Crossword Puzzle

Create a crossword puzzle for a classmate to solve. You may work out your clues in the space below. Use the grid on the next page to make your puzzle.

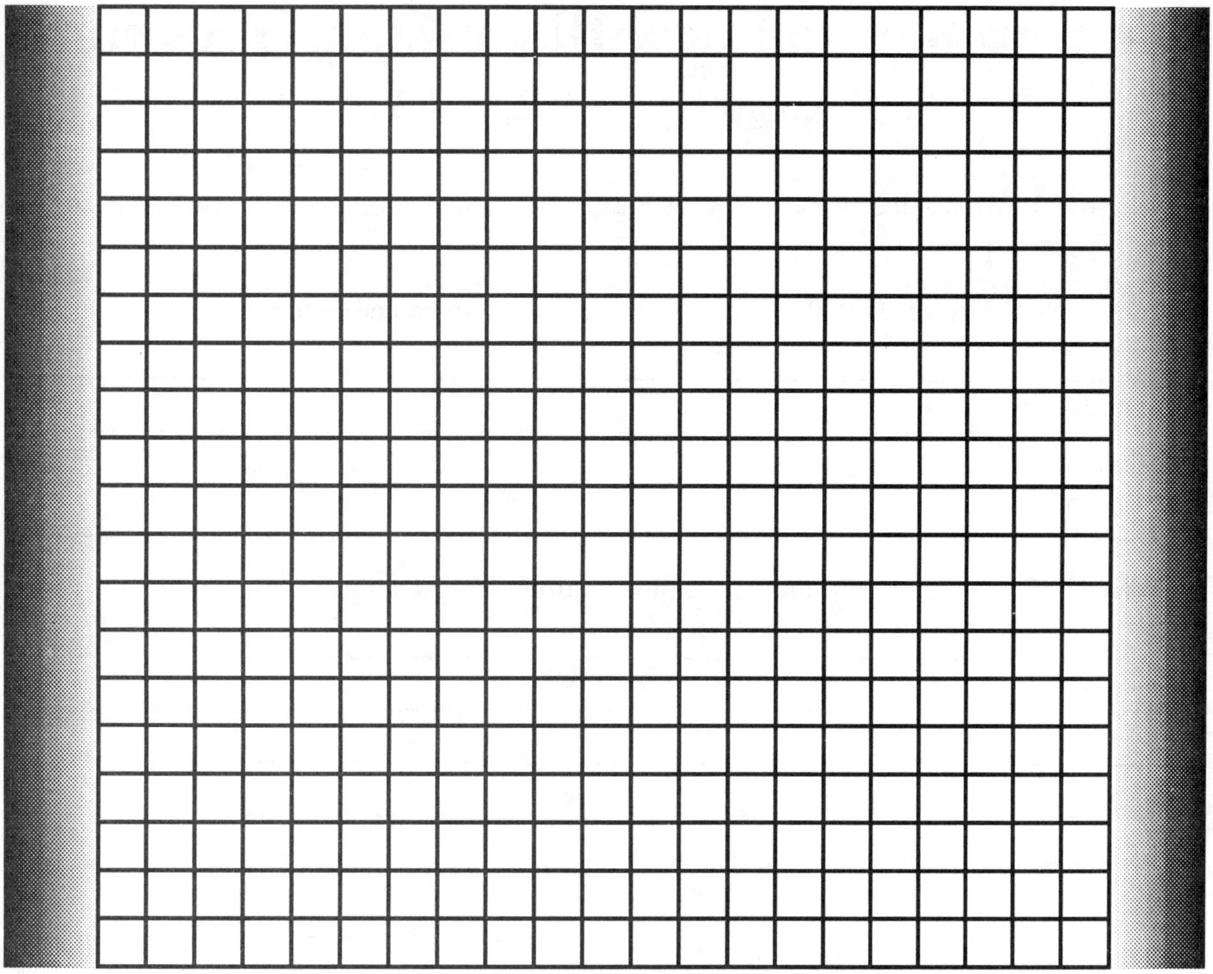

Across

Down

Comprehension and Discussion Questions

Chapters 41, 42, & 43

Answer the following questions in complete sentence form. Give examples from the story to support your response.

1. Why hadn't Zero realized that the sneakers belonged to someone famous?

2. Why did Stanley and Zero move completely around Big Thumb?

3. Why was Stanley happy despite his predicament?

4. Guess why Zero's mother knew the same song as Stanley's father. Why were the words slightly different?

5. Evaluate Stanley's plan for escaping from the camp with riches.

Vocabulary

Chapters 44, 45, 46, & 47

Match the vocabulary words on the left to the definitions on the right. Place the correct letter on each line.

____	1. approach	A. to come closer
____	2. authenticate	B. lawful; legal
____	3. authorization	C. to shrink from; to wince
____	4. briefcase	D. needing much effort
____	5. custody	E. lacking in stability or security
____	6. flinch	F. sanction; permission
____	7. grimly	G. speaking loudly or violently; raving
____	8. hallucination	H. state of being held under guard
____	9. initiate	I. to move quickly in a disorganized way
____	10. legitimate	J. to begin
____	11. precarious	K. to guarantee to be genuine
____	12. ranting	L. extreme; utter
____	13. scramble	M. a portable case used to carry papers or books
____	14. stark	N. a false perception of objects or events that seems real
____	15. strenuous	O. dismally; gloomily

Choose five vocabulary words from the above activity. Use each in a sentence of your own.

____

____

____

____

____

Comprehension and Discussion Questions

Chapters 44, 45, 46, & 47

Answer the following questions in complete sentence form. Give examples from the story to support your response.

1. Why did Stanley nearly gag on the cereal?

2. Find the excerpt that shows how Kate Barlow's prediction to Trout and Linda Walker came true.

3. The Warden said that the campers wouldn't have to dig any more holes if they didn't talk to anyone. Why didn't she care if any more holes were dug?

4. Why was there an attorney at Camp Green Lake looking for Stanley? What story did the Warden tell her when she returned?

5. What surprising proof did Zero find that proved that the suitcase belonged to Stanley and not to the Warden? Why was it even more surprising that Zero found it?

Vocabulary

Chapters 48, 49, & 50

Use the words in the box to complete the following sentences. You may need to use your dictionary.

access	**anxious**	**caviar**	**comprehend**	**detainees**
hysterical	**incarcerated**	**jurisdiction**	**patent**	
promissory notes	**pursuant**	**subtle**	**tedious**	**urgency**

1. Andrew was _______________ about tomorrow's math test.
2. When she heard the bad news, Mrs. Jones became _______________.
3. Dan didn't understand the _______________ hints we gave.
4. Fixing the computer was _______________ work.
5. Long ago, prisoners were _______________ in dungeons.
6. There was no _______________ to the doctor appointment.
7. Sheriff Clark had no _______________ in the next county.
8. The students did not _______________ the deeper meaning of the poem.
9. Report cards will be issued _______________ to the school handbook.
10. Donna applied for a _______________ for the new car wax formula she developed.
11. Many people consider _______________ a delicacy.
12. The _______________ were being held for political reasons.
13. John would have to pay a lot of money when his _______________ came due.
14. Marcia was denied _______________ to the classified material.

Write an Ad

Using as many vocabulary words as possible, write an ad for *Sploosh.*

____

____

____

Comprehension and Discussion Questions

Chapters 48, 49, & 50

Answer the following questions in complete sentence form. Give examples from the story to support your response.

1. How did the other boys react to Stanley's release? What does it tell you about them?

2. Why was Zero released with Stanley?

3. In Chapter 49 we learn that onions saved Stanley and Zero from the lizards. Explain.

4. Stanley's father invented his foot spray the same day that Elya Yelnat's great-great-grandson carried Madame Zeroni's great-great-great-grandson up the mountain. Explain the significance.

5. Guess who the woman was who was fluffing Hector's hair. How, do you think, did Hector find her?

Cooperative-Learning Activity

Finding Humor

Although *Holes* is a story of crime and punishment, it is easy to find examples of humor at almost every turn of the plot. Author Louis Sachar has cleverly injected humor to soften the seriousness and suspense of the story.

With your cooperative-learning group, look for examples of humor in the story. Allow every member of your group the opportunity to judge what seems funny or absurd. Evaluate your findings, and write the top ten items below. Compare your results with those of other groups.

1. ______________________________

____

2. ______________________________

____

3. ______________________________

____

4. ______________________________

____

5. ______________________________

____

6. ______________________________

____

7. ______________________________

____

8. ______________________________

____

9. ______________________________

____

10. ______________________________

____

Allow class time so that each group can present some favorite humor orally.

Spotlight Literary Skill

Stereotyping

A *stereotype* is a story character with exaggerated personality traits who falsely represents a group of people. Stereotypes exist in many types of literature including fairy tales, folk tales, and legends. The innocent heroine and the wicked villain are both common stereotypes in books. The author of *Holes* has stereotyped some of his characters to make them stand out in the readers' mind.

Read the list of characters below. Next to each name, write one or more personality traits that make the character seem stereotyped.

1. Stanley ______________________________

____

____

2. The Warden ______________________________

____

____

3. Mr. Pendanski ______________________________

____

____

4. Clyde Livingston ______________________________

____

____

5. Stanley's father ______________________________

____

____

6. Zero ______________________________

____

____

7. Derrick Dunne ______________________________

____

____

8. Trout Walker ______________________________

____

____

Spotlight Literary Skill

Palindromes

A *palindrome* is a word, phrase, or sentence that reads the same either forward or backward. Palindromes have been used for many centuries, starting with the ancient Greeks and Romans. In the novel *Holes,* the author has cleverly created a name for the central character that is a palindrome, Stanley Yelnats.

Here are some examples of palindromes that are not in the story.

I. Words

racecar	deed
radar	pop
sees	eye
toot	level

II. Phrases

top spot

III. Sentences

Todd erases a red dot.
Was it a bat I saw?

IV. 2-D Palindrome

GEL
EYE
LEG

Create some palindromes of your own in the space below.

Spotlight Literary Skill

Flashback

Flashback is a literary technique in which the author interrupts the sequence of events to describe events that happened earlier. In *Holes,* Stanley experiences things in the present. The author frequently switches back in time, bringing in a character from the past. Of course, these characters from the past have an importance in the present.

Pretend that you are interviewing the grown-up Stanley Yelnats IV. What questions would you ask about his life since the story ended? Write a list of five questions. Then exchange with a classmate to create possible answers for each.

1. Question: ____

Answer: ____

____

2. Question: ____

Answer: ____

____

3. Question: ____

Answer: ____

____

4. Question: ____

Answer: ____

____

5. Question: ____

Answer: ____

____

Now use an example from the story to illustrate flashback. Explain how the flashback is important to the story of the grown-up Stanley.

____

____

____

____

____

____

Creative-Thinking Activity

Advertising

Stanley's father has finally perfected his sneaker-deodorizing product, Sploosh.

Create an advertising campaign for this new product. For print materials, you may want to design magazine and/or newspaper ads, posters, supermarket circulars, and coupons. You may also decide to write the script for a radio or television commercial. Remember that these are usually very short. To get some ideas, listen and watch some real ads on the radio or television. Analyze them for time, content, casting, animation, and music. Perhaps you'll want to create an advertisement for the internet.

Use the following questions to organize your thoughts.

1. What are the benefits of using this product?

____

____

____

____

2. Why will everyone want to have it?

____

____

____

____

3. What will the package look like?

____

____

____

____

4. How will the effectiveness be demonstrated?

____

____

____

____

Cooperative-Learning Activity

Be an Inventor

After many attempts, Mr. Yelnats invented a solution which deodorizes smelly sneakers. Many successful inventions were created in order to fill a need or to solve a problem. Take a survey of your own needs. Compare your results with those of your cooperative-learning-group members.

1. A household job that I find difficult is ______________________________

____

2. A task at school that could be made easier is ___________________________

____

3. A job that my parents would like to make easier is _________________________

____

Pick a job from your list. Think of a way it could be done better. In the space below, describe how your idea will work. Illustrate your idea. Discuss your idea with your group members.

____

____

____

____

____

Think Like an Inventor!

How could you improve these everyday items? Brainstorm ideas with your group members.

1. a school desk ____

____

____

2. a school notebook ____

____

____

3. a window ____

____

____

Post-Reading Activities
Holes

1. *Holes* was the winner of the prestigious Newbery Award. Use your critical-thinking skills to write an essay that tells why you think the book is or is not worthy of this distinction.

2. Investigate the ways in which the problem of juvenile delinquency is handled in our society. What types of facilities are provided for young offenders? Do the punishments seem to fit the crimes?

3. Divide your class into small cooperative-learning groups. Each group will choose a chapter or section of the story to dramatize. Props may be created to enhance the presentation.

4. Based on the descriptions in the story, draw your own interpretations of the following characters and places: Stanley, Zero, the Wreck Room, the Warden, Camp Green Lake, Mr. Sir, Onion Sam, Kate Barlow, and Madame Zeroni.

5. Make a chart of the connections in the story. Examples: Zero is related to Madame Zeroni. Sam's onions saved Stanley and Zero.

6. Have a classroom invention contest. Judge which invention could be most helpful to students and their families.

7. Write a sequel to *Holes.* Describe what happens next in Stanley's life. Does he ever meet any of the people from Camp Green Lake again? Does the family curse ever reappear? Be sure to add some humor to your story!

8. Stage a mock trial for Stanley. Present witnesses who will discuss his whereabouts at the time Clyde Livingston's sneakers were stolen. Select students to be part of a jury.

Crossword Puzzle

Holes

See how much you remember about *Holes*. Have fun!

ACROSS

6. Kate Barlow was one.
7. Madame _____ put a curse on 16 Across and his descendants.
8. Stanley chose Camp Green Lake instead of this.
9. Zero's real first name.
10. Stanley's nickname.
11. The leader among the "campers."
14. Mr. Pendanski's nickname.
15. Stanley's great-great-grandmother.
16. Stanley's great-great-grandfather.
18. A donkey.
20. Zero wanted to learn to do this.
22. What 16 Across supposedly stole.
23. The onion man.
26. Stanley's father was one.
27. She was looking for treasure.
29. Clyde Livingston's were stolen.
30. Linda Walker's husband.
31. What the guards at Camp Green Lake were called.
32. He often said, "You're not in the Girl Scouts anymore."

DOWN

1. Author's first name.
2. Author's last name.
3. The boys' recreation area.
4. The holes measured _____ feet in all directions.
5. She was beautiful but empty headed.
7. He stole Clyde Livingston's sneakers.
12. Stanley's last name.
13. The Warden's nail polish contained venom from this animal.
17. Derrick Dunne was one.
19. Their bites were deadly.
21. Zero found 16 jars of it.
24. Stanley's lawyer.
25. Clyde Livingston's nickname.
28. Katherine Barlow was known for her spiced ones.

Glossary of Literary Terms

Alliteration: Repetition of initial (beginning) sounds in 2 or more consecutive or neighboring words.

Analogy: A comparison based upon the resemblance in some particular ways between things that are otherwise unlike.

Anecdote: A short account of an interesting, amusing, or biographical occurrence.

Anticlimax: An event that is less important than what occurred before it.

Archaic language: Language that was once common in a particular historic period but which is no longer commonly used.

Cause and effect: The relationship in which one condition brings about another condition as a direct result. The result, or consequence, is called the effect.

Character development: The ways in which the author shows how a character changes as the story proceeds.

Characterization: The method used by the author to give readers information about a character; a description or representation of a person's qualities or peculiarities.

Classify: To arrange according to a category or trait.

Climax: The moment when the action in a story reaches its greatest conflict.

Compare and contrast: To examine the likenesses and differences of two people, ideas, or things. *(Contrast* emphasizes differences. *Compare* may focus on likenesses alone or on likenesses and differences.)

Conflict: The main source of drama and tension in a literary work; the discord between persons or forces that brings about dramatic action.

Connotation: Something suggested or implied, not actually stated.

Description: An account that gives the reader a mental image or picture of something.

Dialect: A form of language used in a certain geographic region; it is distinguished from the standard form of the language by pronunciation, grammar, and/or vocabulary.

Dialogue (dialog): The parts of a literary work that represent conversation.

Fact: A piece of information that can be proven or verified.

Figurative language: Description of one thing in terms usually used for something else. Simile and metaphor are examples of figurative language.

Flashback: The insertion of an earlier event into the normal chronological sequence of a narrative.

Foreshadowing: The use of clues to give readers a hint of events that will occur later on.

Historical fiction: Fiction represented in a setting true to the history of the time in which the story takes place.

Imagery: Language that appeals to the senses; the use of figures of speech or vivid descriptions to produce mental images.

Irony: The use of words to express the opposite of their literal meaning.

Legend: A story handed down from earlier times; its truth is popularly accepted but can't be verified.

Limerick: Humorous 5-lined poem with form *aabba*. Lines 1, 2 and 5 are longer than lines 3 and 4.

Metaphor: A figure of speech that compares two unlike things without the use of "like" or "as."

Mood: The feeling that the author creates for the reader.

Motivation: The reasons for the behavior of a character.

Narrative: The type of writing that tells a story.

Narrator: The character who tells the story.

Opinion: A personal point of view or belief.

Parody: Writing that ridicules or imitates something more serious.

Personification: Figure of speech in which an inanimate object or an abstract idea is given human characteristics.

Play: A literary work written in dialogue form and usually performed before an audience.

Plot: The arrangement or sequence of events in a story.

Point of view: The perspective from which a story is told.

Protagonist: The main character.

Pun: A play on words that are similar in sound but different in meaning.

Realistic fiction: True-to-life fiction; people, places, and happenings are similar to those in real life.

Resolution: Part of the plot (from climax on) where the main dramatic conflict is worked out.

Satire: A literary work that pokes fun at individual or societal weaknesses.

Sequencing: The placement of story elements in the order of their occurrence.

Setting: The time and place in which the story occurs.

Simile: A figure of speech that uses "like" or "as" to compare two unlike things.

Stereotype: A character whose personality traits represent a group rather than an individual.

Suspense: Quality that causes readers to wonder what will happen next.

Symbolism: The use of a thing, character, object, or idea to represent something else.

Synonyms: Words that are very similar in meaning.

Tall tale: An exaggerated story detailing unbelievable events.

Theme: The main idea of a literary work; the message the author wants to communicate, sometimes expressed as a generalization about life.

Tone: The quality or feeling conveyed by the work; the author's style or manner of expression.

Answers

Chapters 1, 2, 3, 4, & 5: Vocabulary

1. forbidden	4. facilities	7. dazed	10. obstacle	13. premises
2. alert	5. counselor	8. gruff	11. hammock	14. perseverance
3. convicted	6. canteen	9. vast	12. embarrassment	

Chapters 1, 2, 3, 4, & 5: Comprehension and Discussion Questions

1. There was no lake. It was not really a camp; it was a detention center.
2. They got to spend a day or two recovering in a tent without having to dig a hole.
3. Answers will vary.
4. The boys would not be able to find water if they ran away.
5. He felt that society will recognize them by their real names when they leave the camp. Answers will vary, but perhaps they based them on physical or mental traits or habits.

Chapters 6 & 7: Vocabulary

1. H	3. K	5. B	7. I	9. M	11. D	13. E	15. J	17. L
2. N	4. F	6. G	8. Q	10. C	12. O	14. P	16. A	

Chapters 6 & 7: Comprehension and Discussion Questions

1. The boys didn't believe him because Clyde Livingston was a big star. It seemed impossible that someone like Stanley could have stolen his sneakers. It was ironic because no one had believed him when he said he was innocent in court. Now no one believed he had stolen them.
2. Stanley was a big fan of Clyde Livingston and was excited to meet him. It made him feel bad that Livingston thought he was a thief.
3. The money from the auction was supposed to go to help the homeless. The judge thought Stanley was taking from the homeless just to get a souvenir.
4. Elya was Stanley's great-great-grandfather. The curse put on him by Madame Zeroni was what seemed to plague Stanley's family.
5. Sarah noticed that "Stanley" was "Yelnats" spelled backward.

Chapters 8, 9, 10, 11, & 12: Comprehension and Discussion Questions

1. A pun is a play on words, sometimes on different senses of the same word and sometimes on the similar sense or sound of different words. The normal term for a recreation room is "Rec Room." "Wreck Room," which sounds the same, was appropriate because everything was broken.
2. It was true that it was his first day, that he had made friends, and that he was tired. It was not true that there was a lake. There was neither swimming nor water-skiing.
3. Stanley thought he would get the rest of the day off for finding a fossilized fish. Some might realize that the Warden had something special in mind.
4. Answers will vary.
5. Except for Zero, X-Ray was the smallest.

Chapters 13, 14, & 15: Vocabulary

1. expert	3. dug	5. cloudiness	7. strained	9. carved
2. inquisitiveness	4. sparkled	6. valuable	8. distrustful	10. seen

Chapters 13, 14, & 15: Comprehension and Discussion Questions

1. He arranged for Stanley to move up one place in the line to get water.
2. She was very tough, flamboyant, commanding, determined, and manipulative. Answers may vary, but she probably wanted them in good condition to keep digging.
3. The Warden had them all go through the dirt twice. She had Zero, the fastest digger, take over X-Ray's hole. She had them make larger holes. She said, "I've waited this long, I can wait another day."
4. X-Ray knew that the Warden spied on them.
5. Answers will vary.

Chapters 16, 17, 18, & 19: Comprehension and Discussion Questions

1. In Chapter 11 we were told that X-Ray really had poor eyesight.

2. In middle school he didn't have any friends. The other kids teased him because he was overweight. Now he had friends (of sorts) and was in much better physical condition.
3. She was only being nice to them because she was using them to find what she was looking for. She was losing patience because they still hadn't found anything. She arrived later and left earlier. She lost her temper and jabbed Armpit with her pitchfork for taking a bathroom break.
4. Answers will vary.
5. Magnet stole Mr. Sir's sunflower seeds. When he threw the sack to Stanley, the seeds spilled into his hole. Stanley took the blame for stealing the sack.

Chapters 20, 21, 22, 23, & 24: Vocabulary

1. pain
2. blame
3. insolence
4. forlorn
5. rude
6. fear
7. extraordinary
8. distorted
9. shock
10. withdraw
11. distant
12. piercing
13. poisonous
14. fierce

Chapters 20, 21, 22, 23, & 24: Comprehension and Discussion Questions

1. Mr. Sir was sure to seek revenge against Stanley for the Warden's treatment of him.
2. He said it was because he wasn't that tired because Zero had dug most of his hole. Perhaps it was also because Zero believed that he was not guilty of stealing the sneakers.
3. Everyone thought Zero was stupid, but he was not. He was especially good at math.
4. Answers will vary.
5. He spilled his water on the ground instead of into Stanley's canteen.

Chapters 25, 26, 27, & 28: Vocabulary

1. asthma
2. remedy
3. blotchy
4. wobble
5. concocts
6. ointment
7. waded
8. digestion
9. semester
10. sparingly
11. motorized

Secret Message: Stanley teaches Zero to read.

Chapters 25, 26, 27, & 28: Comprehension and Discussion Questions

1. The residents of Green Lake were afraid to take chances; therefore, they went to both. Dr. Hawthorn didn't resent this because he himself didn't know which worked. Dr. Hawthorn even tried to cure his own baldness with an onion rub.
2. A mob burned the schoolhouse, accusing Kate of poisoning the childrens' minds with books. Sam was shot attempting to escape being hanged for kissing Kate. Kate was rescued against her will, and Sam's donkey was shot.
3. He knew Mr. Sir had been depriving Stanley of water, so he gave him more whenever he could.
4. His real name was Hector Zeroni. In Chapter 7 we read about Madame Zeroni, who had put a curse on Stanley's family.
5. Answers will vary, but the Warden's description in Chapter 14 and Linda Miller Walker's description in Chapter 28 are very close. The Warden was Trout's descendant. (Note: Miller was also Stanley's great-great-grandmother's name, but no connection was shown.)

Chapters 29 & 30: Vocabulary

1. awkward
2. humid
3. refuge
4. unconscious
5. barren
6. harsh
7. cluster
8. depriving
9. stress
10. delirious
11. astonishment
12. horizon
13. Bravo
14. pry

Chapters 29 & 30: Comprehension and Discussion Questions

1. With the lightning strike Stanley saw an unusual rock formation that resembled a giant fist with the thumb sticking straight up.
2. Mr. Pendanski said Zero was too stupid to learn and that all he was good for was digging holes.
3. She didn't want an investigation.
4. It was a threat regarding Zero. The Warden's nail polish was toxic when wet because it contained rattlesnake venom.
5. Answers will vary, but some will say that Stanley will dig it.

Chapters 31, 32, 33, & 34: Vocabulary

1. E 2. J 3. H 4. C 5. D 6. L 7. B 8. K 9. A 10. F 11. G 12. I

Chapters 31, 32, 33, & 34: Comprehension and Discussion Questions

1. He thought he should have dug his own holes *and* taught Zero.
2. He was a ward of the state. No one cared about him.
3. Answers will vary. He thought Zero might be alive and wanted to save him. If successful, he would have had transportation and water; however, he didn't know how to drive and should have thought about his plan better.
4. He realized that he had to save enough strength for the return trip.
5. Mary Lou was the name of the donkey belonging to Sam, the onion man.

Chapters 35, 36, & 37: Vocabulary

1. height	3. rough	5. dry	7. extending	9. additions
2. germs	4. sharp	6. fragile	8. held	10. timidly

Chapters 35, 36, & 37: Comprehension and Discussion Questions

1. It tasted like peaches. Katherine Barlow had been known for her wonderful spiced peaches before she became an outlaw. Without the sploosh, Zero might have died of thirst; however, it made him ill.
2. Spelling helped take Zero's mind off his pain and weakness.
3. He worried about the pain it would cause his parents if he were never found.
4. The mountain was their last hope. If there was no water, they had no chance of survival. When Stanley saw the weeds and bugs, he knew they were close to water.
5. He said Zero's face looked "like a jack-o'-lantern" that had been left out too long. He compared the sun to a fiery ball, a basketball.

Chapters 38, 39 & 40: Comprehension and Discussion Questions

1. He compared it to a hot fudge sundae.
2. They ate onions and splashed muddy water into their mouths. Big Thumb provided some shade.
3. He confessed that he had taken Clyde Livingston's sneakers. In Chapter 9 Zero had asked if the shoes had red X's on the back. In Chapter 22 Zero said Stanley didn't steal the sneakers.
4. Sam's onion tonic saved her. Mrs. Tennyson said it was caused by bad meat.
5. He didn't realize how far up he had carried Zero.

Chapters 41, 42 & 43: Comprehension and Discussion Questions

1. He couldn't read the sign.
2. They followed the shade.
3. He had acquired a sense of dignity and self-esteem. He now liked himself.
4. Madame Zeroni, Zero's ancestor (probably his great-great-great-grandmother), had taught Stanley's great-great-grandfather the song. Stanley's great-great-grandmother had changed the words to make the lines rhyme.
5. Answers will vary.

Chapters 44, 45, 46, & 47: Vocabulary

1. A 2. K 3. F 4. M 5. H 6. C 7. O 8. N 9. J 10. B 11. E 12. G 13. I 14. L 15. D

Chapters 44, 45, 46, & 47: Comprehension and Discussion Questions

1. It was very sweet. He was used to the bitter taste of onions.
2. "When I was little I'd watch my parents dig holes, every weekend and holiday. When I got bigger, I had to dig, too. Even on Christmas." The Warden was probably Trout and Linda's granddaughter.
3. Now that the suitcase that had been buried by Kate Barlow had been found, there was no need for additional holes.
4. The lawyer was there because Stanley was found innocent and was to be released. The Warden had said that he had been delirious, that he had tried to steal from her, had fallen in a hole, and had been bitten by a poisonous lizard.
5. It had the name Stanley Yelnats on it because it was his great-grandfather's. It was the suitcase stolen from him by Kate Barlow. No one knew that Zero could read.

Chapters 48, 49, & 50: Vocabulary

1. anxious	4. tedious	7. jurisdiction	10. patent	13. promissory notes
2. hysterical	5. incarcerated	8. comprehend	11. caviar	14. access
3. subtle	6. urgency	9. pursuant	12. detainees	

Chapters 48, 49, & 50: Comprehension and Discussion Questions

1. They were happy for him. They were basically nice boys and good friends to one another.
2. Ms. Morengo took him with them because the attorney general could not access Zero's files. They had no record of what he did, how long he was there, or when he was due to get out.
3. The reason the lizards didn't bite them was that they didn't like "onion blood."
4. Years ago Madame Zeroni cursed Elya Yelnat's descendants because he had failed to carry her up the mountain with a stream where the water runs uphill and sing the song to her. In Chapter 38 Stanley carried Zero up the mountain and in the next chapter he sang the song to him. In Chapter 42 we were told that the water seemed to run uphill.
5. She was probably his mother. Stanley had given Hector (Zero) money for a team of private investigators.

Crossword Puzzle:

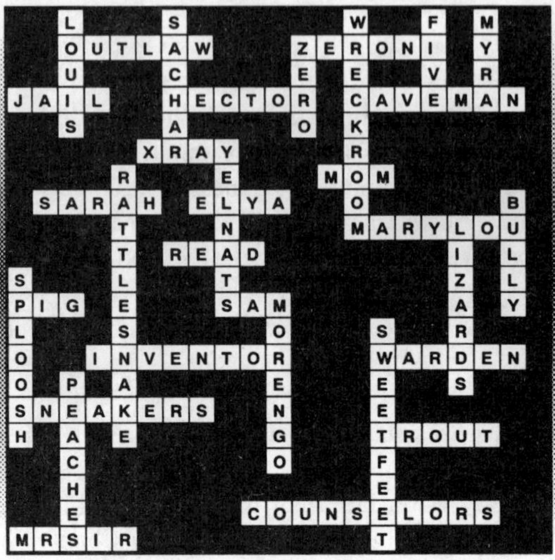

